Reflections on an International Environmental Court

Reflections on an International Environmental Court

Ellen Hey

This text provided the basis for a lecture
given by the author on accepting
the Chair in International Natural Resources Law
at the Faculty of Law of the Erasmus University Rotterdam
on October 6, 2000

Published by:
Kluwer Law International
P.O. Box 85889, 2508 CN The Hague, The Netherlands
sales@kli.wkap.nl
http://www.kluwerlaw.com

Sold and Distributed in North, Central and South America by:
Kluwer Law International
657 Massachusetts Avenue, Cambridge, MA 02139, USA

Sold and Distributed in all other countries by:
Kluwer Law International
Distribution Centre, P.O. Box 322, 3300 AH Dordrecht, The Netherlands

A CIP Catalogue record for this book is available from the Library of Congress

Printed on acid-free paper.

ISBN 90-411-1496-3
© 2000 Kluwer Law International

Painting on the front cover: Mi Desmedt, *Paysage Circulaire 'Le Pommier'*
(for more information see inside back cover)

Photographer: Ed Brandon, The Hague

Typesetting and cover layout by *Steve Lambley Information Design*, The Hague

Kluwer Law International incorporates the publishing programmes of Graham & Trotman Ltd, Kluwer
Law and Taxation Publishers and Martinus Nijhoff Publishers.

These reflections are dedicated to
Janny Hey-Bruinsma, my mother, and
Hendrik Willem Hey, my late father

REFLECTIONS ON AN INTERNATIONAL ENVIRONMENTAL COURT

Introduction

International law governing the settlement of disputes through law-based forums, such as courts, tribunals and arbitral tribunals, is fraught with limitations that are becoming especially apparent with respect to disputes that involve the protection of the environment.[1] The limitations concern, in particular, the non-compulsory nature and the inter-state character of the procedures that are available. However, these limitations are not only becoming apparent in disputes involving international environmental law, but also in disputes involving other areas of international law.[2]

Despite the deficiencies of the law, international courts and tribunals have issued judgements in disputes involving the protection of the environment. At the global level the International Court of Justice (ICJ),[3] the Appellate Body of the World Trade Organization (WTO)[4] and the Tribunal for the Law of the Sea (ITLOS)[5] have handed down decisions in relevant cases.

---

[1] Agenda 21, para. 39.10, identifies the need to make more effective, *inter alia*, procedures for the settlement of disputes, UN Doc. A/CONF.151/26 (Vol. III), 1992.

[2] Francisco Orrego Vicuña and Christopher Pinto, *The Peaceful Settlement of Disputes: Prospects for the Twenty-First Century*, Report Prepared for the 1999 Centennial of the First International Peace Conference, 1999. The authors analyze both the shortcomings of the present system for the settlement of disputes and various proposals for amending that system. The commentaries on the report illustrate significant divergences of opinion as to the way forward. Both the report and the commentaries are available from http://www.minbuza.nl/english/conferences/c_peace_docs.html.

[3] The ICJ, on 8 July 1996, at the request of the United Nations General Assembly, delivered the Advisory Opinion on the *Legality of the Threat or Use of Nuclear Weapons* (*Nuclear Weapons*), ICJ Reports 1996, and, on 25 September 1997, it issued the Judgement in the case *Concerning the Gabčikovo-Nagymaros Project* (Hungary v. Slovakia) (*Gabčikovo-Nagymaros*), ICJ Reports 1997. The cases of the ICJ are also available from http://www.icj-cij.org.

[4] Among the relevant rulings by the Appellate Body of the WTO are *European Community – Measures Concerning Meat and Meat Products* (*Hormones*) cases (United States v. EC and Canada v. EC), 16 January 1998, WT/DS26/AB/R and WT/DS48/AB/R and *United States – Import Prohibitions of Certain Shrimp and Shrimp Products* (*Shrimp – Turtle*) case (India, Malaysia, Pakistan and Thailand v. U.S.), 12 October 1998, WTO Doc. WT/DS58/AB/R. The rulings of WTO panels and the Appellate Body are available from http://www.wto.org.

[5] ITLOS, on 27 August 1999, delivered the Order for Provisional Measures in the *Southern Bluefin Tuna* cases (New Zealand v. Japan (case no. 3); Australia v. Japan (case no. 4)) (hereinafter *Southern Bluefin* cases PM). ITLOS orders and judgements are available from http://www.un.org/Depts/los/ITLOS.

Other legal forums also could be called upon to decide, and some have decided, cases involving international environmental law. Such forums include the Environmental Chamber established by the International Court of Justice in 1993[6] and the Permanent Court of Arbitration (PCA) under its general facilities and under the Environmental Facility that it is planning to establish.[7] Other arbitral procedures also are available to settle disputes involving international environmental law[8] and special bodies, such as the United Nations Compensation Commission (UNCC),[9] may decide on cases involving international environmental law. Moreover, regional forums such as the European Court of Human Rights (ECHR),[10] the Inter-American Court of Human Rights[11] and the Court of Justice of the European Community (ECJ)[12] have

---

[6] Press Release 93/20, ICJ, 19 July 1993. The Environmental Chamber was established on the basis of article 26(1) of the Statute of the Court. Seven judges of the ICJ constitute the Chamber. To date no cases have been brought before the Environmental Chamber.

[7] 99th Annual Report of the Permanent Court of Arbitration, 1999, paras. 80-81 (on environmental facility), available from http://www.pac-cpa.org. Philippe Sands, Environmental Disputes and the Permanent Court of Arbitration: Issues for Consideration, Background Paper for the Secretary-General of the PCA, March 1996 and Philippe Sands and Ruth Mackenzie, Settlement of Disputes under International Environmental Agreements: A Potential Role for the Permanent Court of Arbitration, Background Paper for the Bureau of the PCA, July 1997.

[8] Relevant examples are arbitral tribunals and special arbitral tribunals constituted in accordance with, respectively, Annex VII and Annex VIII of the United Nations Convention on the Law of the Sea (LOS Convention), 10 December 1982, 21 ILM 1261 (1982), arbitral tribunals under the provisions of specific environmental treaties, such as article 27(3)(a) of the Convention on Biological Diversity, June 5, 1992, 31 ILM 849 (1992), and the International Centre for the Settlement of Investment Disputes (ICSID); for further information see http://www.worldbank.org/icsid.

[9] Security Council Resolution 687 (1991), 8 April 1991, (30 ILM 846 (1991)), para. 16, provides that "Iraq … is liable under international law for any direct loss, damage, including environmental damage and the depletion of natural resources … as a result of Iraq's unlawful invasion of Kuwait." The UNCC has classified claims related to environmental damage as category F4 claims. To date no category F4 claims have been decided by the UNCC. Luan Low and David Hodgkinson, "Compensation for Wartime Environmental Damage: Challenges to International Law After the Gulf War," 35 Virginia Journal of International Law 1995, pp. 405-483.

[10] See, for example, the decision of the ECHR in case No. 16798/90 López Ostra v. Spain, 9 December 1994, Series A, vol. 303-C. For examples of other relevant cases decided by the ECHR see Menno Kamminga, "The Precautionary Approach in International Human Rights Law: How It Can Benefit the Environment," David Freestone and Ellen Hey (eds.), The Precautionary Principle and International Law, the Challenge of Implementation, Kluwer Law International, 1996, pp. 171-186; Dinah Shelton, "Human Rights and the Environment," in Yearbook of International Environmental Law, volume 10, 1999, pp. 131-137.

[11] Shelton, ibid.

[12] See, for example, the decision of the ECJ in case C-406/92 [1993] ECR I-6133 (Mondiet). For examples of other relevant cases decided by the ECJ and the role of the ECJ in implementing international environmental law in the European Community see Ellen Hey, "The European Community's Courts and International Environmental Agreements," 7 RECIEL 1998, pp. 4-10.

ruled on cases involving international environmental law.

Despite these developments, calls for the establishment of an international environmental court at the global level persist.[13] Several arguments have been advanced to justify the establishment of an international environmental court.[14] These arguments include the following: the very many pressing environmental problems that we are faced with and the need for a bench consisting of experts in international environmental law to consider these problems, the need for individuals and groups to have access to environmental justice at the international level, the need for international organizations to be able to be parties to disputes related to the protection of the environment and the need for dispute settlement procedures that enable the common interest in the environment to be addressed. Each of these arguments has merit. Whether they justify the establishment of an international environmental court remains to be seen.

Arguments against the establishment of an international environmental court have been advanced as well.[15] These arguments include the following: proliferation of international courts and tribunals would result in the fragmentation of international law, existing courts and tribunals are, or can be, well equipped to consider cases involving environmental issues and disputes involving international environmental law also involve other aspects of international law. Each of these arguments has merit. Whether they justify the retention of the *status quo* also remains to be seen.

In this essay I will explore the arguments for and against the establishment of an international environmental court. My conclusion will be that the establishment of an international environmental court is not the most desirable option. I suggest that it might be more fruitful if we consider developments in environmental law, as well

[13] For example, the Dutch Minister of Housing, Spatial Planning and the Environment, J.P. Pronk, expressed support for the establishment of an international environmental court at the 2nd International Lawyers' Seminar entitled *International Investments and Protection of the Environment: The Role of Dispute Resolution Mechanisms*, organized by the PCA, May 17, 2000, The Hague.

[14] See, among other articles by the same authors, Alfred Rest, "Enhanced Implementation of the Biological Diversity Convention by Judicial Control," 29 *Environmental Policy and Law* 1999, pp. 32-42; Alfred Rest, "The Indispensability of an International Environmental Court," 7 *RECIEL* 1998, pp. 63-67; Alfred Rest, "Need for an International Court for the Environment?," 24 *Environmental Policy and Law* 1994, pp. 173-187; Amedeo Postiglione, "An International Court for the Environment?," 23 *Environmental Policy and Law* 1993, pp. 73-78. Also see the web-site of the International Court of the Environment Foundation http://www.greenchannel.com/icef/.

[15] See, for example, Sir Robert Jennings, then President of the ICJ, in a speech entitled "The role of the ICJ in the development of international environmental protection law," delivered at the United Nations Conference on Environment and Development, reproduced under the title "Need for an Environmental Court?," 20 *Environmental Policy and Law* 1992, pp. 312-314.

as in other relevant areas of international law, from a different perspective, namely, that of administrative law and reassess the relationship between international and national law. This approach is warranted if, inter alia, viable means for resolving environmental disputes that may arise are to be identified.

In this essay I will consider the following topics: the definition of an international environmental dispute and the concomitant expertise required on the bench, fragmentation and its root causes, access to justice and the representation of community interests. I will conclude by suggesting routes that might be pursued both in terms of further research and in practice.

The definition of an international environmental dispute and the concomitant expertise required on the bench

It is beyond doubt that we are facing pressing environmental problems. To name but a few examples: seriously polluted river and ocean waters, grave shortages of water in some areas of the world and overwhelming amounts of water in others, increasing greenhouse gas emissions and diminishing biological diversity.[16] Most, if not all, of these problems are certainly best dealt with through negotiations resulting in preventive and precautionary measures and procedures and conciliatory methods of dispute settlement.[17] However, if disputes do arise and these measures and methods do not provide the desired result, as recent cases have illustrated, international courts and arbitral tribunals do have a role to play.

A question that arises is what types of disputes would be encompassed ratione materae by the jurisdiction of an international environmental court. A relatively simple means of defining an international environmental dispute might be as follows. An international environmental dispute is a dispute that involves what is generally considered to be an environmental treaty as apparent from, for example, the object and purpose of the treaty in question. Besides the well-known problems involved in determining the 'object and purpose' of a treaty,[18] several other problems emerge immediately. First, most, if not all, contemporary multilateral environmental

---

[16] Report of the United Nations Secretary-General, We the Peoples, The Role of the United Nations in the 21st Century, prepared for the Millennium Summit, 2000, pp. 55-65, available from http://www.un.org.

[17] Jutta Brunnée and Stephen Toope, "Environmental Security and Freshwater Resources: Ecosystem Regime Building," 91 American Journal of International Law 1997, pp. 26-59, esp. pp. 44-47.

[18] Isabelle Buffard and Karl Zemanek, "The 'Object and Purpose' of a Treaty: An Enigma?," 3 Austrian Review of International Law & European Law 1998, pp. 311-343; Jan Klabbers, "Some Problems Regarding the Object and Purpose of Treaties," 8 Finnish Yearbook of International Law 1997, pp. 138-160.

agreements aim to foster sustainable development. They thereby explicitly incorporate international development law into the agreement.[19] Second, the operative provisions or additional protocols of multilateral environmental agreements often provide for trade-related instruments to be implemented[20] or for the interests or rights of particular groups, such as indigenous peoples,[21] to be given special consideration. Do these provisions make these agreements into instruments of international trade law or international human rights law? Moreover, how can it be guaranteed that an international environmental court would have the expertise required to consider such trade or human rights aspects? Third, many of the potential disputes that may arise under a treaty that focuses primarily on the protection of the environment also can be defined in terms of a dispute under other treaties. Relevant examples are the United Nations Convention on the Law of the Sea[22] (LOS Convention) and the different treaties annexed to the Agreement Establishing the World Trade Organization.[23]

[19] See, for example, the 16th and 19th paragraphs of the Preamble to the Convention on Biological Diversity, June 5, 1992, and the 20th and 21st paragraphs of the Preamble to the Convention on the Control of Transboundary Movements of Hazardous Wastes and their Disposal (Basel Convention), 22 March 1989, 28 ILM 657 (1989). Also see Jennings, *supra* note 15.

[20] Convention on International Trade in Endangered Species of Wild Fauna and Flora (CITES), 3 March 1973, 12 ILM 1088 (1973); Basel Convention; Montreal Protocol to the Vienna Convention on the Protection of the Ozone Layer, respectively, 16 September 1987 and 22 March 1985, 26 ILM 1541 (1987) and 26 ILM 1529 (1987); Kyoto Protocol to the United Nations Framework Convention on Climate Change (UNFCCC), respectively, December 10, 1997 and May 22, 1992, 37 ILM 22 (1998) and 31 ILM 849 (1992); Cartagena Protocol on Biosafety to the Convention on Biological Diversity, 29 January 2000, http://www.biodiv.org. Neither the Kyoto Protocol nor the Cartagena Protocol have entered into force.

[21] See, for example, 12th paragraph of the Preamble and article 8(j) of the Convention on Biological Diversity.

[22] For example, a dispute related to the emission of land-based sources of marine pollution in the North Eastern Atlantic Ocean under the Paris Convention for the Protection of the Marine Environment of the North-East Atlantic, 22 September 1992, 8 *International Journal of Marine and Coastal Law* 1993, p. 50, could probably be defined in terms of the LOS Convention. In addition, if the pollution originated in a river, such as the Rhine, the dispute could probably also be defined in terms of a convention for the reduction of emissions into that river. In the case of the Rhine this would be the Convention on the Protection against Chemical Pollution, 3 December 1976, 16 ILM 242 (1977) and, when it enters into force, the Convention on the Protection of the Rhine, 12 April 1999, http://home.att.net.

[23] For example, a dispute related to trade in greenhouse gas emission reduction units under the Kyoto Protocol could probably also be defined as a dispute under the General Agreement on Tariffs and Trade or General Agreement on Trade in Services, both 15 April 1994, 33 ILM 1125 (1994). Likewise a dispute related to trade in biologically modified organisms under the Cartagena Protocol could probably be defined in terms of the Agreement on the Application of Sanitary and Phytosanitary Measures, 15 April 1994, http://www.wto.org. For a discussion of the latter possibility see Peter-Tobias Stoll, "Controlling Genetically Modified Organisms: The Cartagena Protocol on Biosafety and the SPS Agreement," 10 *Yearbook of International Environmental Law* 1999, pp. 82-119.

The cases that have been ruled on by international courts and tribunals illustrate the difficulties involved in defining an international environmental dispute. While these cases can all be defined in terms of environmental law and thus potentially could have been brought before an international environmental court, if it had existed, they have another common element. The cases in question also can and have been defined in terms of several other areas of international law. Areas of international law that come to mind are international water law,[24] international human rights law,[25] international fisheries law,[26] international trade law,[27] international law related to the threat or use of force,[28] the law of state succession[29] and international treaty law.[30]

Of interest in this context is a case that Spain brought before the International Court of Justice against Canada.[31] The controversy concerned the conservation and management of fish stocks in the north-western Atlantic Ocean, in which Canada, the European Community and several of its Member States, including Spain, were involved. Canada arrested a Spanish fishing vessel on the high seas based on the argument that the vessel was fishing illegally in that area, contrary to Canadian law and international fisheries conservation obligations applicable to the European Community and therefore to Spain. Canada alleged, inter alia, that, as a result of these fishing activities, marine biological diversity was being threatened. The position of the European Community and Spain was that the international conservation obligations did not apply to the fishing activities in question and that Canada had acted illegally when arresting the vessel. Was this a dispute involving international natural resources law, international fisheries law, international environmental law or international law related to the conservation of biological diversity? Spain presented the case to the Court primarily as a dispute involving an infringement of its rights as

---

[24] Gabčikovo-Nagymaros case, ICJ.

[25] López-Ostra case, ECHR.

[26] Fisheries Jurisdiction case (Spain v. Canada), Jurisdiction of the Court, ICJ, 4 December 1998; Southern Bluefin Tuna cases PM, ITLOS.

[27] See WTO Appellate Body cases referred to in supra note 4.

[28] Legality of the Threat or Use of Nuclear Weapons, Advisory Opinion, ICJ.

[29] Gabčikovo-Nagymaros case, ICJ.

[30] Gabčikovo-Nagymaros case, ICJ; Southern Bluefin Tuna cases PM, ITLOS.

[31] Fisheries Jurisdiction case (Spain v. Canada), ICJ. For information on the dispute see David Freestone, "Canada – European Union / Canada and the EU Reach Agreement to Settle the Estai Dispute," 10 International Journal of Marine and Coastal Law 1995, pp. 397-411.

a flag state[32] – undoubtedly an aspect that was also part of the overall dispute. However, it also is beyond doubt that all of the aforementioned areas of international law would have played a role in deciding the dispute, if the Court had found that it had jurisdiction to consider the merits of the case.

A similar argument can be made with respect to the *Southern Bluefin Tuna* cases PM, between Australia and New Zealand, on the one hand, and Japan, on the other hand, involving the sustainability of fishing activities for southern bluefin tuna in the Pacific Ocean.[33] In this case the Tribunal for the Law of the Sea, on the basis of the LOS Convention, ordered provisional measures requiring Japan to stop an experimental fisheries program on precautionary grounds. The dispute was submitted to arbitration on the merits, administered through the International Centre for the Settlement of Investment Disputes (ICSID).[34] In that procedure Japan contested the jurisdiction of the arbitral tribunal based on the argument that this is not a dispute involving the LOS Convention but a dispute under the Convention for the Conservation of Southern Bluefin Tuna (CCSBT), which does not provide for compulsory dispute settlement.[35] The arbitral tribunal, while not accepting Japan's argument, found that it did not have jurisdiction over the dispute because the dispute settlement procedures in the CCSBT intended to exclude the application of the compulsory dispute settlement provisions of the LOS Convention.[36] Was this a case concerning the law of treaties, fisheries law or environmental law? Furthermore, if the case is defined in terms of environmental law, should we be more precise and determine that it relates to marine environmental law or the conservation of marine biological diversity? Issue involving international fisheries law, (marine) environmental law, the law on the conservation of (marine) biological diversity and broader issues of the law of the sea and of international law generally, including the law of treaties, are obviously at stake,

---

[32] ICJ Press Release No. 95/8, 25 March 1995.

[33] *Supra* note 5. For information on the case see "Symposium: *Southern Bluefin Tuna* Cases Preliminary Measures," 10 *Yearbook of International Environmental Law* 1999, with contributions by Brunnée and Hey, Malcolm D. Evans, Adriana Fabra, David Freestone, Douglas M. Johnston and Francisco Orrego Vicuña, pp. 3-47 and the Report on the decision by Ted McDorman, *ibid.*, pp. 632-635.

[34] ICSID Press Release, May 7, 2000, http://www.worldbank.org/icsid.

[35] Government of Japan, Memorial on Jurisdiction, http:/www.worldbank.org/icsid. The CCBST was concluded on 10 May 1993, http://www.home.aone.net.au. Article 16 and the Annex to the CCBST relate to dispute settlement. Article 16 provides that all parties to a dispute have to agree for a dispute to be submitted either to arbitration or the ICJ.

[36] See press release and text of the decision, dated August 7, 2000, are available from http:/ www.worldbank.org/icsid.

regardless of the forum that considers the dispute. Would an international environmental court have had jurisdiction to consider this dispute, in addition to the various dispute settlement forums referred to in the LOS Convention? According to the LOS Convention, provided the parties to the dispute agreed thereto, an environmental court indeed would have had jurisdiction to consider the case.[37] Would the composition of the bench of an international environmental court guarantee the availability of sufficient expertise in international fisheries law, the law of the sea and the law of treaties for the proper consideration of the case?

Assuming that an international environmental court had been established at the time, would that have meant that the *Gabčikovo-Nagymaros* case,[38] decided by the International Court of Justice, could have been considered by that international environmental court? It probably could have been, given the fact that the sustainable use of the waters of the Danube river, among other issues, was at stake in the case. However, how can we be assured that an international environmental court would have had sufficient expertise to consider the issues of international water law, the law of state succession and the law of treaties, which also were involved in the case?

It also has been argued that, for example, the *Beef Hormones* case[39] and the *Shrimp/Turtle* case,[40] decided by the Appellate Body of the WTO and defined in terms of international trade law, could have been defined, respectively, in terms of international environmental law and the law of the sea[41] and submitted to an international

---

[37] Article 289, LOS Convention provides that Part XV, on the settlement of disputes, does not impair the right of the parties 'to settle a dispute between them concerning the interpretation or application of this Convention by any peaceful means of their own choice'. On the LOS Convention provisions for dispute settlement see E.D. Brown, "Dispute Settlement and the Law of the Sea: the UN Convention Regime," 21 *Marine Policy* 1997, pp. 17-43.

[38] *Supra* note 3. For information on the case see "Symposium: The *Case Concerning the Gabčikovo-Nagymaros Project*," 8 *Yearbook of International Environmental Law* 1997, with contributions by Jutta Brunnée and Ellen Hey, Charles B. Bourne, A.E. Boyle, Paulo Canelas de Castro, Jan Klabbers and Stephan Stec and Gabriel Eckstein, pp. 3-50 and the report on the case by Philippe Sands, ibid., pp. 443-452.

[39] *Supra* note 4. For reflections on the case see Ellen Hey, "Considerations Regarding the *Hormones Case*, the Precautionary Principle and International Dispute Settlement Procedures," 13 *Leiden Journal of International Law* 2000, pp. 239-248. The article suggests, *inter alia*, that this case may also have been defined in terms of health law.

[40] *Supra* note 4. For further information on the case see "Symposium: The *United States – Import Prohibitions of Certain Shrimp and Shrimp Products* Case," 9 *Yearbook of International Environmental Law* 1998, with contributions by Jutta Brunnée and Ellen Hey, Jeffery Attik, Duncan Brack, Jeffrey F. Dunoff, Howard Mann, Thomas J. Schoenbaum and David A. Wirth, pp. 3-47 and the report on the case by Frederick M. Abbott, ibid., pp. 330-332.

[41] See Layla Hughes, "Limiting the Jurisdiction of Dispute Settlement Panels: The WTO Appellate Body Beef Hormone Decision," 10 *Georgetown International Environmental Law Review* 1998, pp. 915-942. Hughes suggests that the WTO DSU does not provide the proper forums for settling disputes involving environmental

environmental court, if it had existed, and the ITLOS. How could we be sure that such an international environmental court and the ITLOS would be well equipped to deal with the trade law aspects of these cases?

Another relevant consideration in this perspective is the integration principle. It has been incorporated into numerous international instruments, both those related primarily to environmental issues and those primarily related to other issues.[42] The integration principle prescribes that environmental considerations are to be incorporated into all other relevant policy areas. Must this be taken to imply that all disputes that arise under such instruments and that have an environmental aspect are to be defined as environmental disputes and therefore are to be submitted to an international environmental court, if it were to exist?

I come to the conclusion that the special character of environmental disputes and the expertise required on the bench to consider such cases do not convincingly argue in favor of the establishment of an international environmental court. The reason is that a dispute that has an environmental aspect also will involve other aspects of international law and vice-versa. The argument that appropriate policies for the composition of the bench of an international environmental court could guarantee the availability of sufficient expertise in other areas of international law has merit, but it is not convincing either. Why not reverse the argument? It should be ensured that existing legal dispute settlement forums are so composed that sufficient expertise in international environmental law is available on their benches.

Fragmentation and its root causes

Several international judges have warned that the proliferation of international courts and tribunals, in the absence of an hierarchy among these forums, risks fragmentation

---

aspects, such as the Hormones case, and that alternative forums should be established. The author does find that a forum that could consider both environmental and trade aspects of a case would be preferable. Richard J. McLaughlin, "Settling Trade-Related Disputes Over the Protection of Marine Living Resources: UNCLOS or WTO?" 10 *Georgetown International Environmental Law Review* 1997, pp. 29-96. McLaughlin suggests that there may be advantages, for a state seeking conservation measures, to bringing disputes regarding the conservation of marine living resources, including those involving unilateral measures such as the *Shrimp/ Turtle* case, before the dispute settlement bodies available under the LOS Convention, rather than submitting such disputes to WTO dispute settlement procedures.

[42] Examples of relevant instruments are the Convention on Biological Diversity (art. 6(b)), the UNFCCC (art. 3(4)), the Treaty Establishing the European Community, as amended on October 2, 1997, (art. 6), 37 ILM 56 (1998), the Rio Declaration on Environment and Development (Principle 4), 31 ILM 874 (1992), and, in a somewhat different version, the Agreement Establishing the World Trade Organization (1st para. Preamble), 33 ILM 1125 (1994).

in the international legal system.[43] They point, *inter alia*, to the divergent conclusions drawn by the International Court of Justice and the European Court of Human Rights on the validity of declarations containing invalid reservations.[44] Reference can also be made to the intricate and intimate connections that exist between many of the cases before the International Criminal Tribunal for the Former Yugoslavia (ICTY)[45] and the case brought by Bosnia and Herzegovina against Yugoslavia before the International Court of Justice,[46] in which the same overall facts and the same legal instruments are at stake.

Other commentators, however, have reacted more positively to the proliferation of international courts and arbitral tribunals and have suggested that a choice of forum is to be welcomed.[47] Both practitioners and academics have pointed out that that the danger of fragmentation should not be over-estimated and can be avoided in practice.[48]

---

[43] Gilbert Guillaume, "The Future of International Judicial Institutions," 44 *International and Comparative Law Quarterly* 1995, pp. 848-862; Gilbert Guillaume, "La Mondialisation et la Cour Internationale de Justice," 2 *International Law FORUM du Droit International* 2000, in press; Sir Robert Jennings, "The Proliferation of Adjudicatory Bodies: Dangers and Possible Answers," *Implications of the Proliferation of International Adjudicatory Bodies for Dispute Resolution*, ASIL Bulletin No. 9, 1995, pp. 2-7; Shigeru Oda, "Dispute Settlement Prospects in the Law of the Sea," 44 *International and Comparative Law Quarterly* 1995, pp. 863-872; Tullio Treves, "Conflicts between the International Tribunal for the Law of the Sea and the International Court of Justice," 31 *New York University Journal of International Law and Politics* 1999, pp. 809-821.

[44] The ECHR in the case *Loizidou v. Turkey* (*Preliminary Objections*), 23 March 1995, http://echr.coe.int, with respect to the declaration by Turkey on the jurisdiction of the court, which contained a reservation regarding the non-application of the Convention to the northern part of Cyprus, held that the reservation was invalid but that the declaration on the recognition of the jurisdiction of the court was valid, only the reservation being devoid of legal effect. The ICJ in its Advisory Opinion in *Reservations to the Convention on the Prevention and Punishment of the Crime of Genocide*, 28 May 1951, ICJ Rep. 1951, however, had held that a state that makes a declaration containing a reservation to which another state party to the Genocide Convention objects can be considered not to be a party to that Convention *vis-à-vis* the objecting state, thereby preventing the declaration from having legal effect. (ICJ Rep. 1951).

[45] For information on the cases before the ICTY, see http://www.un.org/icty.

[46] *Case Concerning Application of the Convention on the Prevention and Punishment of the Crime of Genocide*, General List 91, for various orders and a judgement delivered to date see http://www.icj-cij.org.

[47] Alan Boyle, "Dispute Settlement and the Law of the Sea Convention: Problems of Fragementation and Jurisdiction," 46 *International and Comparative Law Quarterly* 1997, pp. 37-54; Jonathan I. Charney, "Is International Law Threatened by Multiple International Tribunals?," 271 *Recueil des Cours* 1998, pp. 101-373; Jonathan Charney, "The Impact on the International Legal System of the Growth of International Courts and Tribunals," 31 *New York University Journal of International Law and Politics* 1999, pp. 697-708; Krysztof Skubiszewski, "Profile of Professor Krysztof Skubiszewski" by Frances Meadows, 1 *International Law FORUM du Droit International* 1999, pp. 232-236, pp. 235-236.

[48] Georges Abi-Saab, "Fragmentation or Unification: Some Concluding Remarks," 31 *New York University Journal of International Law and Politics* 1999, pp. 919-933; Pierre-Marie Dupuy, "The Danger of Fragmentation or

They propose arrangements for ensuring that sufficient expertise in general international law is available on specialized benches and for frequent consultations among the members of different benches. In addition, they suggest that the International Court of Justice should develop an active judicial policy that would enable it to become, in practice, the principle judicial organ of the United Nations[49] and of the international legal system as a whole.[50] It also has been submitted that '[O]ne strength of the multiplicity of international tribunals is that it permits a degree of experimentation and exploration, which can lead to improvements in international law.'[51]

Other considerations also are relevant. First, the existing international legal system, including procedures for dispute settlement by law-based forums, has developed along functional lines and in an *ad hoc* fashion. As a result, dispute settlement mechanisms have been created within specific regimes, in accordance with the political realities and needs of those regimes and with an eye to the legal framework provided by the particular regime. A systematic approach to the creation of law-based forums for the settlement of disputes has not been developed.[52] This practice has resulted in, *inter alia*, the absence of a hierarchy among the different law-based forums for dispute settlement. Second, many international disputes are in fact non-justiciable because compulsory procedures for settling disputes through law-based forums are the exception, rather than the rule[53] and because major actors on the international scene are excluded from participation in most of the available

Unification of the International Legal System and the International Court of Justice," 31 *New York University Journal of International Law and Politics* 1999, pp. 791-807.

[49] Art. 92 of the United Nations Charter: 'The International Court of Justice shall be the principal judicial organ of the United Nations …'.

[50] On the role(s) of the ICJ see Georges Abi-Saab, "The International Court as a World Court," Vaughan Lowe and Malgosia Fitzmaurice (eds.), *Fifty Years of the International Court of Justice*, Cambridge University Press, 1996, pp. 3-16.

[51] Charney, 1999, *supra* note 47, p. 700. Similarly see, Skubiszewski, *supra* note 47.

[52] Jennings, *supra* note 43, p. 5, where he also cites Judge Shahabuddeen; Nicolas Valticos, in the discussion, *Implications of the Proliferation of International Adjudicatory Bodies for Dispute Resolution*, ASIL Bulletin No. 9, 1995, p. 45.

[53] Judge *ad hoc* Lauterpacht addressed this problem in his separate opinion to the decision of the ICJ on the case *Concerning Application of the Convention on the Prevention and Punishment of the Crime of Genocide* (*Bosnia and Herzegovina v. Yugoslavia (Serbia and Montenegro)*), Further request for the Indication of Provisional Measures, 13 September 1993. Judge *ad hoc* Lauterpacht in paragraph 15 of his opinion provided as follows. 'The possibility must be recognized and accepted that there are a number – alas a very great number – of substantive rights protected by international law which, for want of a suitable jurisdictional link to the Court, cannot be made the subject of consideration and decision by it. This is not the fault of the Court. It is simply a reflection of the present unsatisfactory state of the international legal system – a reflection, many consider, of lack of appropriate political will on the part of States, not a reflection of the shortcomings in the Court. If jurisdiction exists, the Court will exercise it. That, after all, is what the Court is for.'

procedures.[54] These considerations in turn imply that calls for additional law-based forums for the settlement of disputes will persist and that such forums will be established, if states possess the political will to do so. Recent examples of instances in which this route was pursued are the establishment of the International Tribunal for the Law of the Sea,[55] the International Criminal Tribunal for the former Yugoslavia,[56] the International Criminal Tribunal for Rwanda (ICTR)[57] and the dispute settlement procedures under the WTO.[58] In addition, in 1998 agreement was reached on the Statute of the International Criminal Court (ICC).[59] Each of the instruments establishes, or will establish, compulsory binding dispute settlement mechanisms for a particular situation (ICTY and ICTR) or for a particular regime: the law of the sea (ITLOS), humanitarian law (ICC) and trade law (WTO/DSU). These instruments, in the absence of a hierarchical relationship among law-based forums for dispute settlement increase the danger of diverging interpretations of international law emerging, and thus of fragmentation. The source of this danger lies in the fact that the law of the sea, humanitarian law, trade law and other so-called functional bodies of law, are intimately related to general international law and often are intertwined with each other.

Besides divergent interpretations of the law and conflicts of jurisdiction, the absence of a hierarchy among law-based forums for dispute settlement may also have consequences for the manner in which international law can be developed by such forums. This point can be illustrated by the treatment of the precautionary principle by the International Court of Justice, the WTO Appellate Body and the International

---

[54] See the section below entitled "Access to Justice".

[55] ITLOS was established on the basis of Annex VI of the LOS Convention; its inaugural session took place on 18 October 1996. For further information see Shabtai Rosenne, "International Tribunal for the Law of the Sea: 1996-97 Survey," 13 *International Journal of Marine and Coastal Law* 1998, pp. 487-514.

[56] The ICTY was established on the basis of United Nations Security Council Resolution 827 (1993), 31 ILM 1203 (1993); for the Statute of the ICTY see 31 ILM 1192 (1993) or the web-site of the ICTY, *supra* note 45.

[57] The ICTR was established on the basis of United Nations Security Council Resolution 995 (1994); for the Statute of the Rwanda Tribunal see 33 ILM 1602 (1994). For further information see http://www.un.org/ictr.

[58] The dispute settlement procedure for the World Trade Organization was established on the basis of the Understanding on Rules and Procedures Governing the Settlement of Disputes (DSU), Annex II to the 1994 WTO Agreement, 33 ILM 1226 (1994).

[59] Rome Statute of the International Criminal Court, 37 ILM 999 (1998). For further information see "Symposium: The International Criminal Court," 10 *European Journal of International Law* 1998, with contributions by Ruth Wedgewood, Gerhard Hafner, Kristen Boon, Anne Rübesame and Jonathan Huston, Marten Zwanenburg, Antonio Cassese and Paola Gaeta, pp. 93-191. On the ICC and disputes involving international environmental law see Jean-Marie Henckaerts, "Armed Conflict and the Environment," 10 *Yearbook of International Environmental Law* 1999, pp. 188-193, pp. 189-192.

Tribunal for the Law of the Sea in three different cases. The ICJ in the *Gabčikovo-Nagymaros* case in fact applied the precautionary principle in an environmental context, without referring to it in so many words. The WTO Appellate Body in the *Hormones* case, however, refused to accept the principle as a binding principle of law, because, among other reasons, the ICJ had not recognized it as such in the *Gabčikovo-Nagymaros* case. The Appellate Body held 'that the precautionary principle, at least, outside the field of international environmental law, still awaits authoritative formulation' and accompanied this text with a footnote referring to the ICJ decision in *Gabčikovo-Nagymaros*.[60] The ITLOS in the *Southern Bluefin Tuna* cases PM, as the ICJ, also applied the precautionary principle without explicitly referring to it. More interestingly, the ITLOS did not refer to the earlier ICJ or WTO Appellate Body decisions.

How must we evaluate the WTO Appellate Body's deferral to the International Court of Justice? On the one hand, it may be welcomed as a means of avoiding diverse interpretations in a system where no explicit hierarchy between dispute settlement bodies exists.[61] On the other hand, it also means that the development of international law will be dependent on a forum – the International Court of Justice – where compulsory jurisdiction exists only in exceptional cases. This is in contrast to the other forums, where compulsory jurisdiction does exist. It implies that there may be limits to the extent to which the International Court of Justice, in fact, will be able to engage in an active judicial policy, as various commentators have suggested it should.[62]

The danger of the fragmentation of international law, as a result of the existence of various judicial dispute settlement mechanisms, is an inherent element of the contemporary international legal system. Its root causes are to be found in the manner in which the international legal system has developed and in the emphasis that the system places on the voluntary submission of disputes to law-based dispute settlement procedures. It is thus that the system that we work with presents us with a 'Catch 22' situation. Either we accept the danger of fragmentation and remedy the unsatisfactory aspects of the system, probably in a piecemeal fashion, or we accept the unsatisfactory nature of current international dispute settlement law and wait for chaos to dictate a complete overhaul of the system. 'Multiplicity of international tribunals' accompanied by 'a degree of experimentation and exploration,'[63] if regarded in this perspective, might be the more desirable route to pursue. In the meantime, practical arrangements

---

[60] *Hormones* case, WTO Appellate Body, para. 123 and footnote 93 in that paragraph.

[61] Dupuy, *supra* note 48, p. 807.

[62] See *supra* text at and note 48.

[63] See Charney, text at *supra* note 51.

to minimize fragmentation are to be welcomed.

The danger of fragmentation is part and parcel of the present law governing the settlement of international disputes via law-based forums. Unless states explicitly define a hierarchy among such forums, the danger of fragmentation will remain part of the system. Given the present lack of political will to introduce a change of this nature, piecemeal adaptations of the existing system, allowing 'for a degree of experimentation and exploration' point the way towards change. Is the establishment of an international environmental court part of the mosaic? I do not think so. The main reason is that such a court, given its undoubtedly broad jurisdiction *ratione materae*, risks introducing too much competition among law based forums for dispute settlement and thus of fragmentation. It might provoke more 'experimentation and exploration' than the system can accommodate. 'Experimentation and exploration' in my view preferably should be directed at other options.

Access to justice

The calls for access to environmental justice to justify the establishment of an international environmental court have great moral weight. This argument becomes clear given that significant power is exercised by various actors and that such power often is not subject to the rule of law. International organizations, multinational corporations, non-governmental organizations, individuals and states exercise significant powers that are not easily subjected to the scrutiny of either a national or an international court of law.[64] Think, for example, of the difficulties encountered in holding multinational corporations accountable in law for damage resulting from their activities in countries other than their state of nationality – the activities of TEXACO in Ecuador come to mind.[65] Think of how the World Bank, the International Monetary Fund or a donor state might be held accountable in law for any harmful effects that may result from projects that they support and that may cause both social and environmental damage.[66]

In terms of law the calls for access to environmental justice involve at least three distinct issues. First, individuals and public interest groups should be able to hold states accountable in law for the non-observance of international environmental law.

---

[64] Robert Y. Jennings, "The International Court of Justice after Fifty Years," 89 *American Journal of International Law* 1995, pp. 493-505, pp. 504-505.

[65] Case entitled Petroleum in the Ecuadorian Amazon Water Pollution due to Petroleum Exploitation, Proceedings of the International Water Tribunal, vol. entitled *Pollution*, IWT Foundation, 1994, pp. 64-174.

[66] See *infra* text at and notes 82 and 83.

Second, individuals and public interest groups should be able to hold non-state actors, such as multinational corporations, accountable in law. Third, individuals, public interest groups and states should be able to hold international organizations accountable in law.

Before concluding that all these types of situations should be resolved at the international level, careful consideration should be given to the question which of these types of disputes, or which aspects thereof, might more adequately be dealt with through national courts. My tentative conclusion is that both the first and second type of disputes, in principle, can be more adequately addressed through national courts, at least in the first instance.[67] In many countries, this solution will require a reconsideration of the relationship between international (environmental) law and national law.[68] In addition, in order to operate effectively, in a number of states it will require a reconsideration of the rules of access to justice for public interest groups and individuals, also in a transboundary context.[69] Moreover, it should be ensured that national judges are well informed of international (environmental) law.[70] Coordination of such steps at the international level certainly is desirable.[71] Ultimately, an international court of referral or appeal could complete the picture.

---

[67] For a skeptical view on the possible role of national courts in implementing international law see Eyal Benvenisti, "Judges and Foreign Affairs: A Comment on the Institut de Droit International's Resolution on 'The Activities of National Courts and the International Relations of their State'," 3 *European Journal of International Law* 1994, pp. 423-439.

[68] See 7 RECIEL 1998, with contributions by Daniel Bodansky and Jutta Brunnée, Michael R. Anderson, Donald Rothwell and Ben Boer, André Nollkaemper, Jutta Brunnée and Daniel Bodansky on the application of international environmental law by national courts and by Ellen Hey on the application of the same body of law by the European Courts. Rest, *supra* note 14, published in the same issue, also refers to the deficiencies of national courts in applying international environmental law and to the lack of standing granted to public interest groups as a reason for the establishment of an international environmental court.

[69] 3 RECIEL 1994, with contributions by Adriana Fabra Aguilar, Mark A. Scholfield and David S. Thompson, Gerrit Bethlem, Antonio G.M. La Viña, Edesio Fernandes and Martin Lau on access to environmental justice in different states and by Philippe Sands on the same topic in European Community law.

[70] In this respect the UNEP symposia for national judges are to be welcomed, see Lal Kurukulasuriya, "United Nations Environment Programme (UNEP) Regional Symposia on the Role of the Judiciary in Promoting the Rule of Law in the Area of Sustainable Development," 10 *Yearbook of International Environmental Law* 1999, pp. 753-763.

[71] See, for example, the proposed EC Draft Directive on Access to Justice in Environmental Matters, prepared by the Öko-Institut, in cooperation with the Foundation for International Environmental Law and Development (FIELD). Although the proposed Directive was removed from the agenda by the European Commission, it provides an apt illustration of the type of coordination that could be pursued at the international level. For the text of the proposed draft Directive and the accompanying report see 3 *RECIEL* 1994, pp. 261-267.

Such a court could have a role similar to either that of the Court of Justice of the European Community when issuing preliminary rulings[72] and/or to that of the European Court of Human Rights as a court of last resort.[73] The references to these two courts and their work illustrate that the above considerations are not unique to disputes involving international environmental law.

The topic clearly requires further research. However, significant steps in that direction have and are being taken, also in the Netherlands. Several national legal systems offer possibilities to hold multinational corporations accountable, also for activities conducted outside their state of origin, as has been illustrated by the research project on multinationals conducted during the past three years by Menno Kamminga[74] and Saman Zia Zarifi[75] at the GLODIS Institute of the Faculty of Law of the Erasmus University Rotterdam (EUR).[76] In addition, Professor André Nollkaemper, a former colleague at the EUR and now at the University of Amsterdam, recently has initiated a major research project in which the prospects for enforcing international law through national courts are being thoroughly researched.[77] Given this initiative I will not dwell any further on these two aspects of the calls for access to environmental justice and await the results of ongoing research.

The third aspect merits further attention here. It is the call for, in particular, individuals and public interest groups, but also states, to be able to hold international organizations accountable in law. Its relevance becomes apparent when one reflects on the role that such organizations have taken on in international relations and the effect that their activities may have on individuals, groups and states.[78] Think, for example, of the situation, much commented on, where the World Bank issues a loan

---

[72] Art. 234 (ex art. 177) ECT.

[73] Art. 35, Protocol 11 to the European Convention on Human Rights, 11 May 1994, 33 ILM 943 (1993).

[74] The research project was initiated by Menno Kamminga, now Professor of Public International Law at Maastricht University.

[75] Saman Zia Zarifi now works with Human Rights Watch in New York.

[76] The results of the project have been published in various articles and in M. Kamminga and S. Zia-Zarifi (eds.) *Liability of Multinational Corporations under International Law*, Kluwer Law International, in press, 2000.

[77] For further information on the project see http://www.jur.uva.nl/acil/pionier/index.htm.

[78] Daniel Bodansky, "The Legitimacy of International Governance: A Coming Challenge for International Environmental Law?," 93 *American Journal of International Law* 1999, pp. 596-624. More in general see Moshe Hirsch, *The Responsibility of International Organizations Toward Third Parties*, Martinus Nijhoff Publishers, 1995 and the recent work of the Committee on the Accountability of International Organisations of the International Law Association (ILA), First Report by Co-Rapporteurs Malcolm Shaw and Karel Wellens, ILA, *Report of the Sixty-Eighth Conference*, 1998, pp. 584-608.

to build a large dam, which results in the displacement of large groups of persons and damage to the environment.[79] In those cases a factual relationship exists between the international organization, in this case the World Bank, and the individuals and groups that are affected by the project. That factual relationship, however, is not translated into a concomitant legal relationship in international law. Instead, international law merges the interests of the individuals and groups with those of their state and creates a relationship in law between that state and the international organization.[80] Nevertheless, even if a dispute arises within that relationship, the dispute, in most cases, is not justiciable; only political and diplomatic means are available for its settlement. The following examples illustrate this point. Which actor could be held accountable in law for any negligent conduct of the United Nations/NATO/Dutch troops during the atrocities committed by Serb troops in Sebrenica?[81] How can the International Monetary Fund be held accountable in law for, for example, any detrimental effects that the implementation of its economic restructuring programs may have on the social security arrangements in a country?[82] How can the World Bank be held accountable in law for its participation in the Chad-Cameroon oil and pipeline project, if that project were to result in environmental or other harm?[83]

The call for the development of mechanisms to hold international organizations accountable in law is problematic because it addresses a basic assumption of the traditional international legal system. That assumption is that international organizations do not exercise powers independently of their member states. As the above-mentioned examples illustrate, this assumption has become a fiction, even if in a formal legal sense member states have not transferred powers to the organization in

---

[79] See, for example the web-site of the World Commission on Dams http://www.dams.org. On the position of international development banks and international law and sustainable development see Günther Handl, "The Legal Mandate of Multilateral Development Banks as Agents for Change towards Sustainable Development," 92 *American Journal of International Law* 1998, pp. 642-665.

[80] Also see Philip Allott, "The International Court and the Voice of Justice," Lowe and Fitzmaurice (eds.), *supra* note 50, pp. 17-39.

[81] Report of the United Nations Secretary-General pursuant to General Assembly Resolution 53/35, *The fall of Sebrenica*, 15 November 1999, GA Doc. A/54/549.

[82] Ongoing doctoral research project conducted by Gerhard Anders on Social Security in Malawi: The Effects of International Standards and Structural Adjustment Programs (supervisors: Keebet von Benda-Beckmann and Ellen Hey).

[83] S.A. Bronckhorst (ed.), *Laibility for Environmental Damage and the World Bank's Chad-Cameroon Oil and Pipeline Project*, Netherlands Committee for IUCN, 2000.

question. The assumption, however, still finds a strong reflection in the law on the settlement of international disputes via law-based forums.

The dispute settlement procedures before the International Court of Justice,[84] the International Tribunal for the Law of the Sea[85] and the dispute settlement forums of the World Trade Organization,[86] are, with minor exceptions, not accessible to individuals, groups or international organizations. The exceptions, both derived from the LOS Convention, are of interest here. First, natural and legal persons, including states, have access to the Sea-bed Disputes Chamber of the International Tribunal for the Law of the Sea for purposes of holding the International Seabed Authority accountable, and vice-versa, in cases involving activities in the Area.[87] The second exception, although not of a compulsory nature, relates to the fact that the International Tribunal for the Law of the Sea is open to 'entities other than States Parties ... in any case submitted pursuant to any other agreement conferring jurisdiction on the Tribunal which is accepted by all the parties to the case.'[88] These exceptions illustrate that access to international law-based forums for dispute settlement can be made available to non-state actors through international law.

The General Assembly and Security Council of the United Nations as well as specialized UN agencies, duly so authorized by the General Assembly, may request the International Court of Justice to deliver an advisory opinion.[89] The Council and Assembly of the International Seabed Authority likewise may request such an opinion from the Sea-Bed Disputes Chamber of the International Tribunal for the Law of the Sea.[90] An advisory opinion, however, does not constitute a legally binding ruling and, more importantly, its use is at the discretion of the international organization. Also relevant in this context is the fact that the International Court of Justice to date has declined to submit decisions by organs of the United Nations to judicial review.[91]

---

[84] Art. 34, Statute ICJ. On the ICJ and international organizations see D.W. Bowett, "The Court's role in relation to International Organizations," Lowe and Fitzmaurice (eds.), *supra* note 50, pp. 181-192.

[85] Art. 20(1), Annex VI, LOS Convention.

[86] Art. 1, DSU.

[87] Art. 187, LOS Convention.

[88] Art. 20(2), Annex VI, LOS Convention.

[89] Art. 96, Charter of the United Nations and Arts. 65-68, Statute of the ICJ. Rosalyn Higgens, "A Comment on the Current Health of Advisory Opinions," Lowe and Fitzmaurice (eds.), *supra* note 50, pp. 567-581.

[90] Arts. 159(10), 191, and art. 40(2), Annex VI, LOS Convention.

[91] *Certain Expenses of the United Nations*, Advisory Opinion, 20 July 1962, ICJ Rep. 1962, p. 151 and *Legal Consequences for States of the Continued Presence of South Africa in Namibia (South-West Africa) notwithstanding Security Council Resolution 276 (1970)*, 21 June 1971, ICJ Rep. 1971, p. 16. Also see Krysztof Skubiszewski, "The International

The European Community, as an organization, may appear as a party in cases before various international law-based forums for dispute settlement, including the International Tribunal for the Law of the Sea and WTO dispute settlement forums. This option is related intrinsically to the fact that the Member States of the European Community formally, in terms of law, have transferred competences in certain policy areas to the Community.[92] Such a formal transfer of competences has not occurred between the states that are members of international organizations and those organizations. Furthermore, in those cases where the European Community appears as a party in cases before, for example, ITLOS or WTO dispute settlement forums, it is not individuals or groups that can hold the Community accountable, but only other parties to a given treaty. The role of the Community, in such cases, is more akin to that of a state at the international level, than that of an international organization.

Interesting in the context of European Community law is the fact that European Community law offers the possibility for natural and legal persons to hold the Community and its institutions accountable, without requiring the consent of the parties to the dispute.[93] The limitations of this route for individuals and public interest groups seeking access to environmental justice have been well documented: the European Courts, to date, have not recognized public interest groups or individuals as interested parties in cases involving environmental law between such parties and Community institutions.[94]

There also are various arbitration facilities in which individuals, groups, multinational corporations and international organizations and states can participate.[95] Noteworthy in this respect are the rules of the Permanent Court of Arbitration on arbitration in international disputes between two parties, of which only one is a state, and similar rules for disputes involving intergovernmental organizations and states and international organizations and private parties.[96] Effective access to justice for individuals and groups vis-à-vis international organizations, however, requires that the procedures be compulsory in nature and not dependent on the will of the

---

Court of Justice and the Security Council," in Lowe and Fitzmaurice (eds.), *supra* note 50, pp. 606-629 , esp. pp. 623-627.

[92] Court of Justice of the European Community in *Costa v. ENEL*, Case 6/64 [1964] ECR 585.

[93] Art. 230(4) (ex article 173) and art. 232(3) (ex art. 175), ECT.

[94] J.H. Jans, H.G. Sevenstern and H.H.B. Veder, *Europees Milieurecht in Nederland* (European Environmental Law in the Netherlands), Boom Juridische Uitgevers, 2000, pp. 294-297.

[95] For example, ICSID, *supra* note 8.

[96] Available from the web-site of the PCA, *supra* note 7 and in Permanent Court of Arbitration, *Basic Documents*, 1998.

parties to the dispute, and especially not on the will of the more powerful party involved, *i.e.* the international organization. This is the problem that arises in respect of the available arbitration procedures, all of which are dependent on the will of the parties to a dispute, including the international organization.

The examples referred to in this paragraph illustrate two points. First, law-based forums for the settlement of disputes in which international organizations have a role and in which individuals and public interest groups can hold international organizations accountable can be conceptualized in international law. Second, in practice, a bleak picture emerges where the accountability of international organizations is concerned. Few law-based forums exist at the international level through which individuals, public interest groups or states can hold international organizations accountable in law. Moreover, where such forums do exist, with one exception,[97] the consent of the international organization is required before it can be held accountable.

A solution might be emerging with the establishment of the Inspection Panel by the World Bank[98] and similar institutions by other development banks.[99] These procedures, although of a quasi-legal nature, translate factual relationships that exist between individuals and groups and an international organization into a legal relationship, albeit of a quasi-legal nature, and enable the individuals and groups to hold the organization accountable. In this context it is also interesting to note that the International Monetary Fund will be establishing an Independent Evaluation Office.[100] At the time of writing, however, it seemed unlikely that this body will be entitled to hear complaints from affected individuals or groups.[101]

The arguments related to access to justice strongly argue in favor of the reconsideration of the relationship between international and national law, for the establishment of an international court of referral or appeal and for the establishment of forums in which international organizations can be held accountable. They do not, however, in my opinion, present a strong argument in favor of the establishment of an international environmental court. This is so mainly because such a court runs the risk of being

---

[97] See text at note 87.

[98] For information on the Inspection Panel, its report and its operating procedures see http://www.world bank.org/html/ins-panel. Also see Ellen Hey, "The World Bank Inspection Panel: Towards the Recognition of a New Legally Relevant Relationship in International Law," 2 *Hofstra Law and Policy Symposium* 1997, pp. 61-74.

[99] Both the Asian Development Bank and the Inter-American Development Bank have established inspection panels. For further information see http://www.ciel.org.

[100] IMF Press Releases No. 00/27, April 10, 2000, and No. 00/49, August 18, 2000, and background paper, *Review of Experience with Evaluation in the Fund*, March 14, 2000, available from http://www.imf.org.

[101] Action Alert and Fact Sheet on an Evaluation Unit in the IMF, on file with author.

too far removed from the persons most concerned, namely the individuals and groups who are likely to bring claims before it. Moreover, as the complaints submitted to the World Bank Inspection Panel illustrate, where the accountability of international organizations is at stake, complaints are likely also to involve aspects that extend beyond environmental issues. Aspects that come to mind are the proper participation of the local population in the decision making-process, the compensation of displaced persons and the rights of indigenous peoples.[102]

Community interests

The interests of all members of the international community may be at stake in case of environmental deterioration. For example, greenhouse gasses emitted somewhere on earth may result in damage anywhere on earth. Moreover, in many situations a causal link between an activity and harm suffered may be difficult to establish. The climate change problem may serve to illustrate this point: greenhouse gasses are emitted everywhere on earth and any resulting damage, in, for example, the form of global warming, cannot be readily traced to any one specific source of emissions. The same is true for emissions of ozone-depleting gasses and any damage that may result on earth as a result of the depletion of the ozone layer. In the case of the conservation of biological diversity, all states and individuals also have an interest in the protection of that diversity, given that its conservation is crucial for life on earth.

In those cases where community interests are at stake, in terms of law, we are concerned with the *erga omnes* character of the environmental rules. During the last few years the recognition has gained ground that many rules of international environmental law, as well as rules in other areas of international law, may have an *erga omnes* character, but the notion remains problematic.[103] This is the case especially with respect to the law regarding law-based means for the settlement of international disputes, where the *actio popularis* is not generally available.[104] Why is this the case?

---

[102] See, for example, Benedict Kingsbury, "Operational Policies of International Institutions as Part of the Law-Making Process: The World Bank and Indigenous Peoples," Guy S. Goodwin-Gill and Stefan Talmon (eds.), *The Reality of International Law, Essays in Honour of Ian Brownlie*, 1999, pp. 323-342 and the World Bank Inspection Panel reports available from its web-site, *supra* note 98.

[103] On obligations *erga omnes* in general see Maurizio Ragazzi, *The Concept of International Obligations Erga Omnes*, Clarendon Press, 1997, (paperback edition 2000); on obligations *erga omnes* and international environmental law see Ragazzi, *ibid.*, pp. 154-162.

[104] On this point see Christine Chinkin, *Third Parties in International Law*, Clarendon Press, 1993, esp. pp. 282-288; Ragazzi, *supra* note 103; E. Valencia-Ospina, "The International Court of Justice and International

As discussed in the previous section, the traditional system of international law recognizes only relationships between states as legally relevant. It constructs those relationships as bilateral relationships.[105] As a corollary to that construction, dispute settlement mechanisms were designed for states, the submission of disputes to adjudication is dependent on the agreement of the states concerned and the procedures are of an inter partes and adversarial nature, not even facilitating the representation of third party interests.[106] This means that the traditional international legal system is more easily compared to systems of national private law[107] than to systems of national administrative law or public law, especially where law-based forums for dispute settlement procedures are concerned.[108] This is the systemic problem that is the source of the difficulties encountered with the representation of community interests in international procedures for dispute settlement.[109]

Judge Weeramantry, then Vice-President of the International Court of Justice, in his Separate Opinion to the decision of the court in the Gabcikovo-Nagymaros case, referred to this problem in the context of international obligations regarding the environment. He states that

> An important conceptual problem arises when, in such a dispute inter partes, an
> issue arises regarding an alleged violation of rights or duties in relation to the
> rest of the world. The Court in the discharge of its traditional duty to decide
> between parties, makes the decision which is in accordance with justice and fairness
> between the parties. The procedure it follows is largely adversarial. Yet this scarcely

Environmental Law," speech delivered at the 31st session of the Asian-African Legal Consultative Committee, Islamabad, January 1992, reproduced in 2 Asian Yearbook of International Law 1992, pp. 1-10, p. 3.

[105] Christine Chinkin, supra note 104, pp. 1-7.

[106] Ibid. pp. 147-288.

[107] H. Lauterpacht, Private Law Sources and Analogies of International Law (with special reference to international abitration), Longmans, Green and Co., 1927.

[108] Judge ad hoc Lauterpacht referred to this problem in the context of criminal law in his Separate opinion in the case Concerning the Application of the Convention on the Crime of Genocide (Bosnia Herzegovina v. Yugoslavia) on the admissibility of counterclaims, ICJ, 17 December 1997, para. 23. Judge ad hoc Lauterpacht stated as follows: 'The closer one approaches the problems posed by the operation of the judicial settlement procedure contemplated by Article IX of the Genocide Convention, the more one is obliged to recognize that these problems are of an entirely different kind from those normally confronting an international tribunal of essentially civil, as opposed to criminal, jurisdiction. The difficulties are systemic and their solution cannot be rapidly achieved …'.

[109] Richard Bilder already addressed this aspect of the problem, as well as others, in 1975, in his lectures at the Academy of International Law, see Richard Bilder, "The Settlement of Disputes in the Field of the International Law of the Environment," 144 Recueil des Cours 1975 (I), 1976, pp. 140-239, pp. 230-232. Also see Allott, supra note 80.

does justice to rights and obligations of an *erga omnes* character – least of all in cases involving environmental damage of a far-reaching and irreversible nature. I draw attention to this problem as it will present itself sooner or later in the field of environmental law, and because (though not essential to the decision actually reached) the facts of this case draw attention to it in a particularly pointed form.[110] (italics in original)

He subsequently suggests that '*inter partes* adversarial procedures … may need reconsideration in future' and that in addressing problems that concern the greater interests of humanity and planetary welfare, 'which transcend the individual rights and obligations of the litigating States, international law will need to look beyond procedural rules fashioned for purely *inter partes* litigation.'[111] Judge Weeramantry furthermore states that

> The great ecological questions now surfacing will call for thought upon this matter. International environmental law will need to proceed beyond weighing the rights and obligations of parties within a closed compartment of individual State self-interest, unrelated to the global concerns of humanity as a whole.[112]

Whether the problems involved in representing community interests in judicial and arbitral procedures can be adequately resolved by the introduction of the *actio popolaris* for states in international law requires further consideration. This is because it may be doubted whether states in all relevant cases are likely to use such a right, given their overall interests in their mutual relationships.[113] It is thus that we return to the issue of access to justice, discussed in the preceding section. The reluctance of states to take each other to court presents an argument in favor of the establishment of improved access to justice at both the national and the international levels. The inspection panel procedures established by international development banks may provide lessons to be learnt in this respect. In addition, the establishment of an independent body that could hold international organizations and states accountable should also be considered. Depending on how it develops, the Independent Evaluation

---

[110] Separate opinion Judge Weeramantry, p. 25.

[111] *Ibid.*

[112] *Ibid.* p. 26.

[113] On the reluctance of states to use dispute settlement procedures in international environmental law see Patricia W. Birnie and Alan E. Boyle, *International Law & the Environment*, Clarendon Press, 1992, pp. 136-187; in international law in general see Peter Malanczuk, *Akehurst's Modern Introduction to International Law*, 7th edition, Routledge, 1997, pp. 300-305.

Office to be established by the International Monetary Fund also may offer useful insights.

A particularly relevant type of procedure in this context is the non-compliance, or compliance, procedure established, or in the process of being established, within multilateral environmental agreements.[114] While various reasons have been advanced for the creation of such procedures, it can be argued that, in the absence of effective dispute settlement mechanisms, they are a means of holding states accountable for the implementation of their obligations undertaken on the basis of the treaty in question, if not vis-à-vis the community of states, at least vis-à-vis the community of states parties to the treaty in question. As is the case with the inspection panel procedures, the non-compliance procedures also are of a quasi-legal character. However, if we view them as an early phase in the development of international administrative law, we might find relevant points of reference for the development of international law-based procedures for the settlement of disputes, including those disputes that involve environmental law. I believe these routes to be viable and to represent a degree of 'experimentation and exploration' that can and will be accommodated by the international legal system. In addition, as Judge Weeramantry, suggests the inter partes nature of law-based dispute settlement procedures in existing forums should be reconsidered.

Conclusions

Disputes involving environmental issues are of a special character in that they aptly illustrate the intricate relationship that exists between different so-called functional areas of international law and general international law. Whether we consider the implementation of the precautionary principle or the principle of common but differentiated responsibilities, social and economic considerations and, thus, human rights law and international economic and development law, play a role. The integration principle translates this notion into the legal system.

The danger of fragmentation is a consequence of the present law governing the settlement of disputes through law-based forums. Ideally that body of law should be amended by the establishment of an explicit hierarchy among international law-based forums for the settlement of disputes, with at the top of the system a court

---

[114] Maas M. Goote, "Non-compliance Procedures in International Environmental Law," 1 *International Law FORUM du Droit International* 1999, pp. 82-89; by the same author, "Non-Compliance Procedures," in 9 *Yearbook of International Environmental Law* 1998, pp. 146-158 and in 10 *Yearbook of International Environmental Law* 1999, pp. 155-179.

with an appeal and/or referral function. This step, however, is more easily formulated than translated into practice. At least for the time being, changes in the body of law governing dispute settlement will have to be introduced in a piecemeal fashion, through 'experimentation and exploration.' The establishment of an international environmental court, in my view, is not the preferred route to pursue, as it would, given the effect of the integration principle, augment the danger of fragmentation by causing too much competition among international law-based forums for the settlement of disputes.

The need to enhance the rule of law through access to justice and the representation of community interests are the core of the arguments for the establishment of an international environmental court. Their implications, however, extend well beyond disputes involving international environmental concerns. They relate to the relationship between international and national law and to the origins of the international legal system as inter-state law. They also require a reassessment of the international legal system, or at least parts thereof, in terms of administrative law. It is at these aspects that reforms of the law on the settlement of disputes should be directed, also if disputes involving environmental issues are to be addressed more adequately in the future. This aspect of the calls for the establishment of an international environmental court should be recognized for what they are: calls for the introduction of the rule of law and justice into international relations.

The approach advocated here requires a more systematic approach to the establishment of international courts and arbitral tribunals, both in practice and research.

This approach should consider the role that national courts can play in the implementation of international law and the role for an international court of appeal or referral. It should include such procedures as the inspection panels established by international development banks and the compliance procedures established under numerous multilateral environmental agreements.[115] The argument that these types of procedures are of a quasi-legal nature and therefore non-judicial has merit. This is so especially because the forum deciding on accountability and the policy-making organs are closely intertwined. However, we must remember that this has been the case for other earlier forms of dispute settlement procedures in national administrative law. It was, after all, only in 1985 that the European Court of Human Rights with its ruling in the case *Benthem v. Netherlands*[116] induced the overall

---

[115] Kingsbury, *supra* note 102.

[116] The case *Benthem v. Netherlands*, 23 October 1985, Series A, vol. 97.

reorganization of the administrative court system in the Netherlands. In its decision the Court held that the Dutch administrative court system, at the time, was too close for comfort to the executive branch of government for it qualify as an independent and impartial judicial procedure, at least for purposes of article 6(1) of the European Convention on Human Rights.[117]

How should we regard the initiative of the Permanent Court of Arbitration to establish an Environmental Facility in this perspective? I suggest that in the future it will be regarded as a welcome element of the 'experimentation and exploration' that characterizes the introduction of change into the international legal system at the beginning of the 21st century. While the Environmental Facility is unlikely to result in essentially new procedures, compared to the procedures already available at the PCA,[118] it may well result in increased confidence in the PCA as a platform for settling disputes involving international environmental issues and thus in more disputes being settled in practice. Another example that involves experimentation is a proposal that is being discussed within the framework for the elaboration of the Kyoto Protocol. It envisages, still in square brackets, the establishment of an enforcement branch that could take decisions with legally binding consequences, as part of the non-compliance procedure for the Protocol,[119] a step that hitherto has not been envisaged as part of a compliance procedure.

Experimentation and exploration, especially, should play a more important role in academic research. More innovative research on the settlement of disputes, including disputes involving environmental issues, should be initiated. I invite in particular those specialized in administrative law to join with international lawyers in the development of a discourse on international administrative law and concomitant dispute settlement mechanisms.

The international legal system, including its rules on dispute settlement, has not been amended to accommodate to the societal changes that evolved during the second half of the 20th century. These changes are best characterized by the terms 'globalization', 'interdependence' and 'transnational relations'. Many of the transnational relations that exist in fact, however, have not been translated into law. The

---

[117] N. Verheij, "De toegang tot de rechter in het bestuursrecht," (Access to court in administrative law), R.A. Lawson and E. Myjer, *50 Jaar Europees Verdrag voor de Rechten van de Mens* (50 Years European Convention on Human Rights), Special issue NJCM-Bulletin, vol. 25, no. 1, 2000, pp. 183-201.

[118] Also see Sands, *supra* note 7, para. 110-115.

[119] Annex to Procedures and Mechanisms Relating to Compliance under the Kyoto Protocol, Doc FCCC/SB/2000/CRP.3/Rev.1, June 5, 2000, available from http://www.unfccc.org.

challenge for the first decades of the 21st century is to develop the legal system, both national and international, so that those factual relations are captured in terms of law, including the law governing law-based means for dispute settlement. But I doubt whether an international environmental court should be part of the solution.

Acknowledgements

I thank the Board of Directors of the Erasmus University Rotterdam, the Erasmus Trustfund and the Faculty of Law, in particular Dean Hans De Doelder, for facilitating my appointment as Professor of International Natural Resources Law.

I thank Paul Wenting, my student assistant, for helping me gather the materials for this essay and for the good humor with which he approached my very many demands for photocopies of yet another article or chapter.

I thank Philomene Verlaan for the very useful editorial suggestions that she made for the text of this essay.

I also thank Mi Desmedt for allowing me to select one of her very many beautiful works of art for the cover of the publication of this essay.

I especially thank all those who over the years and on life's very many different paths have inspired my curiosity and taught me that the source of inspiration, also for teaching and research, is captured in the words 'I do not know.'[120] Dear Keebet, dear Professor von Benda-Beckmann, I thank you for joining me in exploring many routes unknown to both of us. Dear colleagues and students, I will continue to explore the many routes that 'I do not know' and invite you to join me on those paths.

Frits, although law, and especially international natural resources law, takes up much of my time, you have taught me that the following thought is essential if those resources and their environment are to be conserved.

> The countryside surrounding my home is mine. According to the lawyer, not a blade of grass belongs to me, but I am allowed to wander among the nettles and thistles. I continuously watch right in front of my feet, so that I harm nothing of what I value. I love daisies more than the window of a jeweler's shop.[121] (translation E.H.)

---

[120] Wislawa Szymborska, "De Dichter en de Wereld," (The Poet and the World), Speech delivered at the acceptance of the Nobel Prize for Literature, 7 December 1996, *Einde en Begin, Gedichten 1975-1997* (End and Beginning, Poems 1975-1997), Meulenhoff, 1999, pp. 291-295.

[121] Jopie Huisman, *Schilder van het Mededogen* (Painter of Compassion), De Toorts, 1996, p. 119.